On your "**March**", get set, go!

Surviving Tough Times

Adrienne M. Allen
(MsUnderstood Adrienne)

On Your March, Get Set, Go

SURVIVING TOUGH TIMES

Copyright © 2021 by Trient Press

All rights reserved. No part of this publication may be reproduced, distributed, or transmitted in any form or by any means, including photocopying, recording, or other electronic or mechanical methods, without the prior written permission of the publisher, except in the case of brief quotations embodied in critical reviews and certain other noncommercial uses permitted by copyright law. For permission requests, write to the publisher, addressed "Attention: Permissions Coordinator," at the address below.

Criminal copyright infringement, including infringement without monetary gain, is investigated by the FBI and is punishable by up to five years in federal prison and a fine of $250,000.

Except for the original story material written by the author, all songs, song titles, and lyrics mentioned in the novel The Silent Wars are the exclusive property of the respective artists, songwriters, and copyright holder.

Trient Press
3375 S Rainbow Blvd
#81710, SMB 13135
Las Vegas,NV 89180
Ordering Information:
Quantity sales. Special discounts are available on quantity purchases by corporations, associations, and others. For details, contact the publisher at the address above.
Orders by U.S. trade bookstores and wholesalers. Please contact Trient Press: Tel: (775) 996-3844; or visit www.trientpress.com.
Printed in the United States of America
Publisher's Cataloging-in-Publication data
Author Name- Allen, Adrienne M.
A title of a book : SURVIVING TOUGH TIMES

ISBN
Hard Cover   978-1-955198-33-2
Paperback 978-1-955198-35-6
E-book   978-1-955198-34-9

Contents

Dedication
Introduction
- Day 1: What It Means to Survive
- Day 2: The Philosophy of Whosoever-Wills
- Day 3: You cannot stop being God's instrument.
- Day 4: The way we march matters
- Day 5: What to seek forgiveness for
- Day 6: How important is God in your life?
- Day 7: How to stop limiting your blessings
- Day 8: The best way to invite blessings into your life
- Day 9: Returning to the miracle of the ordinary
- Day 10: Eliminate anxiety by understanding God and time.
- Day 11: All limits are placed by mortals.
- Day 12: Why we talk differently about God
- Day 13: The global average breath: understanding potential.
- Day 14: Everything must exist together.
- Day 15: Empathy paves the way for generational prosperity
- Day 16: Those you help must want to be helped.
- Day 17: Base nature vs. spiritual nature: What is your truth?

Day 18: If you can make a difference, you should make a difference.
Day 19: Belief is having the courage to speak and the patience to listen
Day 20: The significance and reality of Jesus
Day 21: Learn something different, and it will make all the difference
Day 22: Understand that God is grand.
Day 23: Lessons learned talking to a Muslim about Jesus.
Day 24: How to turn your life into a feel-good movie
Day 25: If you're good at being bad, the enemy will be mad.
Day 26: What we are fighting: uncertainty and threats to faith.
Day 27: How to be on your march
Day 28: How to get set.
Day 29: How to go.
Day 30: God Got Goons - Is That You?
Epilogue: You always have a home
About The Author

Dedication

This book is dedicated to everyone breathing. Remember how important every breath we share is another persons' air. Existing together allows our children to live in a world under Gods' care. In addition, thank you to my only son, Chris for being exactly who you are. To my parents, thank you for life. My upbringing was tough, but I can stand today with nothing to say other than "I thank you."

Introduction

For a long time since the rapid acceleration of the tech industry, scientists have pondered ways to replace humans. The peak of this endeavor has been the emergence of artificial intelligence. However, scientists discovered that there is no way to create natural intelligence without having it embodied. In other words, for you to perceive a handle, you must have hands. For you to perceive taste, you must have a tongue.

Without perception, there is no experience, but without embodiment, there is no perception. This discovery only brings home the depth of the idea of our savior embodied in Jesus Christ. For Him to perceive humanity and all its flaws before deciding that we are worth forgiving and worth the sacrifice is an idea that must carry more weight today.

In addition to there being no perception without embodiment, it turns out, there is no process in the absence of belief. In other words, for a robot to help wash your dishes, it must be programmed with the belief that dishes are worth washing. If robots can't exist without a goal, how can humans? I don't believe atheists worship any God because science has all but proven that what one pursues as his top priority is his God. For some this is money, for others, this is a celebrity.

It isn't in your words that you declare your God but in your pursuit that you reveal your God. I do not attempt to convert atheists with this book, but I do my best to serve my community with the reminder that we must return to Christ not in words but in actions. Let this be a journey in the renewal of belief and your commitment. I am hoping that as you turn each page, you get more steadfast in your willingness to stick to the values of Christianity.

These values are larger than any institution or person and how deeply you resonate with them is not for anyone else to judge. We all need saving, and no individual can say you are any less worthy of it because of your past, your income status, your race, or even the frequency with which you worship.

This book is about finding power in Christ and facing challenging times with the love of our Lord and Savior. You do not need to be any particular type of person to derive this benefit, you don't even need to be Christian.

As long as you can share the love, embody the values, and have faith, you can face the storms of uncertainty and come out better, and stronger on the other side. Each chapter is meant to be read in a day. This way, 30 lessons will accompany you as we walk through this month where you can meditate on one tiny step towards self-improvement. As you spend this month with me, I urge you to reflect deeply and avoid the desire to remain complacent. I wish you all the best for this exciting journey.

Day 1:
What It Means To Survive

It all starts with the story you tell yourself versus the story you tell others. If you think about surviving, you look at surviving and think, I already did it. I've done this, I have conquered it, I have made it through it. I am done! You've already survived only to find that you are right back in the same situation, still understanding that not too far in the near future, you'll be trying to figure out how have you ended up in the same situation again. Today is a day to hear me and hear me well. You have survived! We have survived! We must survive, and show our children what it looks like to do so.

In this book, "Surviving Tough Times", you will be able to really understand how to have the best day, and your worst day all in the same day. It happens to the best of us and if you have looked up and become one of us, I'd say that this book is your journey. You're not only going to get to know you. You will understand why God made you. With a better understanding you find that you start to understand other people, and how God made them as well. This allows you to realize, they too have survived.

What does it mean to survive?
I would have to say that in 2020, we have survived COVID-19. Although we lost a lot of lives there are still people breathing. We also have been victimized by senseless violence and we've lost a lot of lives to racism masked as hatred. We've lost a lot of lives, so today we need to realize that we have truly survived.

What is it to survive is a question that hundreds of years from now may even be a moot point. Today let us all begin to realize that we have survived. We are surviving, it's all we must do in appreciation of our Creator. The fact that we were created allows us the opportunity to embrace everyone in their differences. We will learn to live together in harmony so that our children's children's children have a better example than what they are seeing today.

I encourage you for this first day to just sit back and think how many things have you already survived. These tough times will come and go but as long as there is still air coming through your lungs, and out your nose, you are breathing. You should know that God has your back, and if you didn't know that, start today. Make today a day of knowing that what we have done is survived, and what you are doing is surviving. God has allowed all of it to happen and when we leave this earth it will be said, "You survived a lot so keep on surviving". Just remember this is only the beginning. Good luck to you. I look forward to seeing you on the other side. Let this month be a real genuine ride that no one can do better than you. Above all, you deserve everything that God has coming to you.

Your Thoughts

Day 2:
The Philosophy of Whosoever-Wills

If you know about my Radio Show, D-Block Church, you may have some familiarity with the term "Whosoever-Wills." In this chapter, I uncover the philosophy behind why I aim to bring the love of Christ to the Whosoever-Wills.

Who are the whosoever-wills?

Let's start by defining the term. I consider anyone who can breathe a whosoever-will. In other words, I aim to bring the love of Christ and His message to anyone regardless of their race, income, and, yes, even religion. Whosoever is quite literally, whosoever. This is because our Lord is abundant and we have made the mistake of limiting His love, forgiveness, and message to our biases.

We have become like the person who discovers a well in a drought-ridden town and decides to build a wall around it. Do you feel positive about this person? Not really, but, then why do you hold back loving someone in Christ Jesus? As far as love and empathy are concerned, the world right now is as drought-ridden as is possible.

People are starved of love and are forced to live a life of base pursuits and sad material pleasures. They are judged more than they are appreciated, scolded more than they are soothed, and hated more than they are loved. This only furthers the cycle because humans are reactionary. One person hating another creates at least three haters.

In that we can find hope, if the hatred of two can create three haters, what can the love of a million do? I truly believe we can create a revolution by selling ourselves on the philosophy of whosoever-wills.

Gratitude for the discovery.

Just being born is a gift. Did you know that the odds of you being born are one in four hundred trillion? You got that lucky to be born, but considering the sixteen religions currently on the leader board, your odds of being born and then discovering Jesus are six thousand four hundred trillion. If you won the lottery (one in fourteen million odds), you'd be incredibly thankful and may even give money to charity as a gesture of gratitude.

Where is the gratitude for seeing the light? Where is the gratitude for finding Jesus? Gratitude isn't saying "Thank You, Lord" while attempting to hoard His love to the group you decided is more worthy of a blessing. By being grateful, you show love by extending it to your neighbors even if they are Hindu. Gratitude is evident by extending His love to your coworker even if he is Muslim.

The philosophy of whosoever-wills is a philosophy of resonating with the Lord's abundance. It is the belief that you can channel love and let it flow through you without your human biases limiting it one bit. Today, I urge you to make a list of all the people in your life to whom you have not extended love and empathy. Please don't hold back. As long as they breathe, they're worthy, and if they're worthy, you're worthy. Stop being harsh on others so you can go easy on yourself.

Your Thoughts

Day 3:
You Cannot Stop Being God's Instrument

When something apparently negative happens in your life, what do you do? Do you panic? Do you feel bad? Do you scramble around to find a sudden fix? In this chapter, I will show you the general human method of operating in the face of negative incidents. Once you have an idea of how that works, you'll learn about a stronger alternative.

You see yourself as an instrument for yourself. I know that subheading is a mouthful but hear me out. Let's say you have a job and you have a savings goal. Who is making money to get to your goal? You. Let's suppose you want to surprise your boyfriend. Who is planning the surprise? You. Humans are goal-seeking beings and as a result, we see ourselves as a part of our plans. This is why whenever something "bad" happens, we get annoyed.

Imagine packing up your hammer to go for your carpentry gig only to open your pack and find dish-washing soap. You wouldn't be pleased. The misplaced tool is the culprit. Similarly, in your plans, be it a short term or a long term plan, when you don't find yourself where you need to be the most effective, you get angry or discouraged. Guess what? You are always in the right place as far as God's plan is concerned. If you relate to that more than you relate to your own plan, you'll not find yourself feeling bad.

What it is like being God's instrument.
It is not your choice whether you want to be God's instrument or not. Even the most popular atheist preachers who spread doubt are God's instrument to test our belief. Even those who act negatively are his instrument because they're the ones who provide you the opportunity to rise above it all. If you cannot help but be God's instrument regardless of what you do, why not get intentional about it?

In becoming intentional about being God's instrument, you no longer play the side-role in the larger narrative of life. You become one of the main characters. Things don't happen to you, they happen for you. Whenever something seemingly negative happens, it's because God wants you to take an alternative path or learn something new. Above all, you become abundant in your thinking and more positive in your approach to life.

In conclusion, I want you to make this day a day of reflection on your plans. Understand that your plans are made from the limited perspective of a human. Know that God has bigger plans and where your plan and His plan overlap, you will find joy. Even where Gods' plan differs, you will be fine. He will take care of you. Think about the last few times you thought something horrible was going to happen. Did something bad happen? You're fine now. You have survived everything "bad" that has happened to you. Thank the Lord for it, and be prepared to trust Him.

Your Thoughts

Day 4:
The Way We March Matters

My rallying cry in 2020 has been "On Your March, Get Set, Go." I swapped march for marks because, in a race, you run as individuals, but my God Got Goons community is moving forward together. It's not a race, it's a march of progress, peace, and prosperity. It is a mission to improve the conditions of the whosoever-wills by extending the love of Jesus to every human whose life we touch. In this chapter, we will go over the significance of perception because perception creates reality.

How we march affects who we march with.

You may have heard the phrase, "Birds of a feather flock together." That seems to be universally true. Royals hang out with royals, techies hang out with techies, and so on. That is why, when we march with biases, judgment, a holier-than-thou attitude, we don't fill our ranks with people genuinely dedicated to the mission. Our ranks, instead, are filled by those who want to pat themselves on the back for having a love of Christ to the exclusion of others. We fill our ranks with elitists and those interested in barriers, not boundlessness.

How we march creates or eliminates confusion.

If we march with a message of love but hate those who disagree with us, we create confusion. In the corporate world, everyone knows that confused messaging leads to billion-dollar failures. Companies – no matter how big – can fail, but our mission is too important for us to do so. We must succeed in engulfing the planet with love and empathy. For that, we must march with clarity. We must know our message, profess the same message, and then act it out in the world.

How we march creates reality.

With even the surface-level knowledge of Genesis, most people know that God speaks things into being. This power of the word is not so direct in humans. We speak things into perception, and if we stick with the perception, we turn it into reality. "Fake it till you make it", is an atheistic concept because the atheist doesn't trust his word. We know that we can speak words into perception and turn them into our reality. It is a genuine, noble, creative process. You cannot speak things into existence if your actions counter the perception. So when you march with a message of love and faith, you must act such that the perception of faith and love is upheld.

Today, make a list of all the areas in which you can embody love and show more faith. Faith in the process, faith in yourself, and faith in Christ. Write down at least ten things you can do better with more
love and faith, and when you improve yourself, you are marching with my community. You are a part of my community. We are all improving ourselves. We all have faith. We all love each other in Christ and just like I won't judge you for your circumstances, conditions, and decisions, I hope you extend the same courtesy to the whosoever-wills in your life.

Your Thoughts

Day 5:
What To Seek Forgiveness For

At the time of writing this, it is evident that the Democrats have won the presidential election. Many in the community resonate with democratic values of social giving and community welfare. On the other hand, the president since 2016 has become a symbol of polarization and brashness. It is easy to rationalize hatred when someone like that is in power for so long. It is tempting to gloat, but I want this to be a sobering moment for our community. I want us to seek forgiveness for having ill will towards a man in his seventies.

It is great to conquer and I want to congratulate everyone who wanted to vote him out, you have accomplished what you set out to do. You did not let life happen to you. You took matters into your own hands and made a difference in a legal and legitimate way. It is good to conquer, but gloating is a display of milking the victory. Guess who milks something for every ounce, the one with the scarcity mindset.

A billionaire never negotiates on his grocery bill because he does not want to milk a dollar for every bit of material value. Why? Because he has a billion more of those coming. I want you to have that expectation in regards to victory. Don't stop and gloat as if this is the only win you will experience in your life. There's a good chance you're reading this when 2020 seems like far off history, and who was the president matters not one bit. The lesson still stands: whatever victory you experience, act like it is one of a thousand more coming your way.

The first benefit of this is in pure optics, you do not repel people you have won against. You soon shift from winning against people to winning over their hearts. The second benefit is that you move forward instead of getting stuck. It is easy to get stuck on a win and let time make you a loser. If you had a million dollars and you kept it in a safe, it would eventually become worth less than a thousand bucks. If money cannot afford to stay in one place, how can you and I?

In victory, move forward with grace and avoid losing momentum. In defeat, avoid resentment, seek forgiveness for the animosity and ill-will. "They deserve it!" you may be tempted to protest, but remember, we are no one to pass that judgment.

It would take an incredible coincidence for us to have dispensed exactly as much ill will as someone "deserves." If you have wished harm on someone, repent. If you have felt joy in someone's suffering, repent. If you have hoped someone goes through or stays in pain, repent.

Today is the day you take losses less personally. Remember that yesterday, you acknowledged that you are an instrument of God regardless of how your life goes. Take defeats as detours and victories as jumping-off points. Stop neither to gloat nor to harm. Peace.

Your Thoughts

Day 6:
How Important Is God In Your Life?

We have always worshiped different deities on different levels of organization of our species. Let that sink in. It is possible for a family to be Hindu, but you to be a Christian individual in it. On the family level, in this case, the unit worships Hindu gods. Similarly, it is possible for your entire family to be Christian but be residing in a Muslim country.

I believe this hierarchy goes all the way up to the planet level. In the times of the Roman Christian empire, we worshiped our God on the highest level of organization. Today, Christianity is the largest religion, and that should imply that we still worship God on the planet level, but that isn't evident from our actions and public conversations.

It seems like there are two Gods competing for global worship: money and individual rights. Those who preach the gospel of infinite rights pursue individualism and discard all the blessings that come with cooperation, cohesion, and organization. Those who pursue money, to the exclusion of all else, confine themselves to a material experience instead of a spiritual one.

Believe me, I am not against accumulating wealth, I'm against worshiping it. As mentioned in the introduction, your God in practice is whatever your highest aim is. So, aim towards spreading the love and message of Jesus Christ and get your money as if it is your right because, you'll earn what is coming to you. However, ask yourself how important God is in your life.

Track the time you spend at your job or in your business chasing money. Compare that with the time you spend praising the Lord and sharing His love. You will see a contrast that doesn't paint a pretty picture. Notice how the conversations you have about brands, stocks, relationships, and money all flow together but the moment you bring up God, the conversation changes. That is the tragedy of trying to compartmentalize God.

When you confine God and His blessings to a box, you automatically prioritize everything else over Him. You cannot spend 24 hours in a church. Even if it is D-block Church, you cannot have it in your ears for

24 hours. So the best way to make sure you spend a majority of your time with God is to bring Him into everything else.

You will know that God is integrated into your life when you can talk about Him with as much ease as you talk about your husband or your sibling. What are those? Relationships. When your relationship with Jesus is as natural as a conversation it becomes effortless as well.

So make today the day where you set the strategy to ease God into every area of your life. When you earn so you can spend the money experiencing God's blessing, your money pursuits become a Christian act. When you multiply your wealth so you can bless others, your investments become Christian. When you hang out with your friends and can have conversations about Christ, your social life becomes Christian. When everything you do leads back to Christ, your God in practice becomes the one who created you. I hope every Christian can do this so our planet as a whole can return to Christ in practice.

Your Thoughts

Day 7:
How To Stop Limiting Your Blessings

There have been several experiments on entitlement and as it turns out that people set their price-anchors around their history and their asks around their self-worth. The person with high self-worth demands the stars and gets the moon. The one with low self-worth feels like a fraud getting paid what he deserves. Many salesmen talk themselves out of a sale only because of how little they internally believe what they deserve.

In this chapter, I am going to remind you that God is infinite, and so are His blessings. This will be a reminder that you do not have to limit your prayers and asks by what you think you deserve. Ask from God whatever your heart desires. You do not need to be bound by the social programming around you, but to get access to the limitlessness of God, you must fulfill one simple condition: Do not put God in a box.

We have a tendency to put things in a box just to make sense of them. Don't believe me? Okay, tell me who Michael Jackson was? "A Singer," you'll likely say, but the man had hundreds of hobbies, I am sure. He was an art collector, he was a father, and he was a son. However, we need to put him in a box just to make sense of him in relation to our lives. He's a singer to us because we listen to his songs.

Now that may be fine with celebrities, bosses, and coworkers, however, when we put God in a box we fail to give Him the priority that is His right. Most of us put God in a box of worship and keep His will separate from every other area of life. Some of us even limit His blessings to a particular faith or even a denomination within a religion. God is limitless! His love is not bound by our opinions. You cannot think, believe, or act a certain way that would change God's love. Humans are not powerful enough to affect God. God is loving, and that will not change. You can extend God's love to a fellow Muslim, Hindu, or Sikh because their positions do not make God any less loving.

When you stand by this idea, you tell your subconscious that God is infinite, and doing this on a regular basis raises your sense of what you ask of God, and what you expect from Him. Let today be the day where you accept God without limits and decide to let go of any prejudices that may have limited your ability to serve Him or extend His love. Write down ten ways in which you have imposed some limitation on your opinion of God. Once you have listed these, write what you can do to correct this. If you have only ever asked for enough to survive the next month, pray to get enough to bless others. If you have only shared love and empathy with your church members, extend it to the cashier at your local store even if you don't know her religion. Let today be a revelation.

Your Thoughts

Day 8:
The Best Way To Invite Blessings Into Your Life

God's blessings are infinite, and yet a finite number of humans seem not to be getting all that they desire. This math doesn't add up. I have hope for the future and believe there shall be a time where we all will have all that we desire, and the planet will be engulfed in gratitude and positivity. We must first fix the problem that is creating this lack all around us. This is not a problem on God's end. There will never be a problem on God's side.

The issue is in how we ask. We ask from God the same way we ask from humans. That means we have an upper-limit in mind when we approach God. Just like a teenager doesn't ask his father for a billion dollars, we don't ask God for a billion dollars. You can see the discrepancy, that youth's dad has a limit to how much he can provide, God has infinite treasures. So why is the attitude of asking the same?

Let's consider another scenario. You are at a supermarket. You bought a bunch of groceries only to pat your pocket and notice you didn't bring your wallet along. Fortunately, your best friend is with you, between asking them for the money and asking a stranger, who would you pick? You'd obviously ask your best friend.

Unfortunately, we treat God the same way. We feel more deserving of blessings when we worship regularly and don't even dare ask for anything if we have treated God like a stranger in our lives. Remember, worship isn't a favor. If anything, the opportunity to worship is a gift. So ask from God what you want regardless of whether you have worshiped regularly or skipped the Church for the last decade. Don't base your entitlement on your worship. You deserve His blessings, not because of any favors you have done for your Church. You deserve God's blessings because you are His child. You can do nothing to change that.

Ask God for what you want for yourself and what you want for your friends. Remember that everyone is programmed with the same hesitation. You can be the source for many if you simply dare to ask for more, pray for more, and work for more. Embody a blessed life, so when people want the same blessings as you, point to Christ, this will work more than limiting blessings and insisting someone convert before you love them.

Today is the day you let this expansive right to pray sink in. Write down five of your greatest desires in love. Pen five more desires that have to do with health. Finally, yes, I'm going there, write down your top five money goals. Ask God for each one of them without hesitation. Repeatedly ask till it flows from your tongue as if you are asking for a penny. Remember that as far as God is concerned, giving you a penny more and a billion more are just as effortless.

Your Thoughts

Day 9:
Returning To The Miracle Of The Ordinary

Almost all elitism, racism, and other isms come from where we place our sense of worth. If we identify with our race so much that we start hating other races, we spread negativity. When we identify with our religion so much that we cannot even have a dialogue with those who don't believe, we constrain our numbers. In this chapter, I will urge you to return to what you have in common with every human on the planet, the ability to breathe.

Breathing is the most ordinary thing in the world because it is what we all can do. If you pay attention, it is a miracle possible only by God's greatness. It is God's gift to us, after all. This is also the foundation of my philosophy of the whosoever-wills. This isn't about others who can breathe, this is about you.

Sit down in a room where you are not likely to get distracted. Close your eyes and start taking deep breaths. With each breath, remind yourself that you are worthy because you embody the miracle of life. Let go of any associations that you hold on to in order to feel good. Feel worthy not because of your job title, your income, or your house. Feel worthy not because of your political beliefs or religious ones. Feel worthy because you are human. This is the self-worth that you cannot lose.

What happens when you return to the ordinary?
By doing the exercise above, you return to the ordinary with a sense of wonder that acknowledges the miracle of your being. This is a great feeling. It also changes everyone around you. You are no longer in the rat race of acquiring more branded clothes or shiny jewelry to feel accepted or loved. You don't cling to any group or association to feel worthy. You feel good about yourself just because of who you are, and people around you can sense that.

Soon, they start asking you what has changed your attitude. Tell them you now love yourself for who you are. If they wish to do the same, you can extend this exercise and philosophy to them as well, but if they don't, you don't need to push it. Your sense of worth comes not from converting others, you love yourself for being yourself.

Of course, this is simple but not easy. You will be tempted to cling to what sets you "apart" but that is a losing game. Realize that humans are more alike than they are different. Ultimately the only thing unique about you is your soul. So don't place your pride in a job title millions of other people have. Why feel like you're better than others because of money, when millions of others have more money than you? Feel better about who you are without having to feel superior. That is the secure confidence that attracts people and grows the march forward. Make sure that today you follow along with my breathing meditation and remember to return to the miracle of breathing whenever life seems to get too complicated.

Your Thoughts

Day 10:
Eliminate Anxiety By Understanding God and Time

God was, God is, and God will be, always! While atheists use the size of the universe to tell people they are insignificant, our faith only grows stronger upon acknowledgment of the vastness of God's creation. While our material size in comparison to the universe is awe-inspiring and helps us rise above our problems, it is by understanding God's relationship to time that we can overcome anxieties about our future.

Remember that God always was, He is now, and He always will be. When you trust an entity that exists beyond time, you don't have to worry about time and its surprises. You will be fine. Just have confidence and faith in God. There are only two reasons why you would have less faith in someone's ability to fix your future, you think they lack the will, or you think they lack the ability.

Let's consider companies that have a high turnover. When asked, employees say they are leaving because they don't think the company has job security. What does this mean? It simply means that they don't think the employer is willing to take care of them. There are also resignations based on unpaid salary. Employees don't leave because they didn't get a month's salary. They leave because they believe the company won't be able to pay salaries in the future as well.

While the flawed system makes it okay to assume that of employers and companies, what makes us dare think that way about God? God is willing to take care of you because He loves you. Is there even a question about God's ability to take care of you? The future is uncertain for you, but not for God. Remember, He will always be. He knows what lies ahead for you because He has a plan for you. So do not let the news media and the negative hype derail you from your faith in God and His fruits.

March on with the confidence that your steps are serving an unchanging plan with the best for you at the end and throughout the journey. I understand that this is easier said than done, so I have curated an exercise to help you. This relies on your recall and habit-forming systems to create a framework which you can default to whenever something makes you uncertain about the future.

Take out a pen and paper (Your notes app won't work for this, you must be more engaged). Start writing about the uncertain situations you survived. Have you survived a breakup? Have you gone through a period of unemployment? Did you get out of debt in the past? Write these things down.

You have most likely written this as "I got out of debt." That's fine, but now, I want you to rewrite each one of those things with credit to God. "God helped me get out of debt." "I was uncertain after getting fired, but God took care of me." After you do this, your brain will be in the state of associating the future with God's plan. Do this exercise today and also every time you're feeling anxious about the future. While I encourage doing this initially with a pen and paper, at some point, it will become a habit to have flashbacks of the times God has taken care of you whenever you're unsure about the future. That's where "God was, God is, and God will always be", becomes "God has taken care of me, God takes care of me, and God will always take care of me."

Your Thoughts

Day 11:
All Limits Are Placed By Mortals

The mere existence of abundance is the solution to most problems. So why is it that humans suffer from lack and scarcity? It is because of our obsession with limitations that we can't enjoy or accept abundance. We are unable to make sense of things without placing limits around them. To perceive a plate, you must see where it ends. To know what kindness is, you must understand what it is not. This system of perception is great for the material world and this reality, but it fails us when we deal with God.

Unlike mortal forms, you cannot place limits around God. Even though it might help you perceive Him, it will be an inaccurate image. Unfortunately, we have collectively subscribed to a limited image of God. A God defined by limitations of group belief isn't the true reflection of our Creator. Jesus remembered through the limits of mortal group-think isn't the true reflection of our savior. It is time you rise above the limitations of group belief to invite abundance into your life. More importantly, it is time you connect to God on a personal level by shedding this layer of misunderstanding.

Limiting God's Love
We wouldn't naturally love those who have wronged us. We surely wouldn't love those who disobey us on the regular, but that's how our love is different from the love of Jesus. Then why do we limit divine love the same way? Why do we insist on extending God's love to only those who believe in Him the same way we do? Remember that love comes before acceptance. That's what makes it special. That God loves even those, who haven't accepted Him yet.

Limiting Communication to God
You can talk to me by dialing into my radio show. You can also email me. Whenever you think of getting in touch with me, you're going to think of a way to get in touch. That's how we mortals communicate: through the limits of physics. When we think of getting in touch with God, we don't have to assume similar limitations. That is the beauty of being in the army of the Creator of heaven and earth. You can connect with Him every moment of every day. Church has its esteemed place, but its role is not to be the limiter of your communication with God. In fact, by bringing connectivity to God to every aspect of your life, you

live a more Christian existence.

Let today be the day where you rise above the limitations of group-think. Forget about whatever your community and surroundings have programmed you to believe in terms of limitations. When you connect to God, it is without limitations. So close your eyes and think about every way you have let group-think limit your perception of God. Have you limited your requests from God? Have you assumed exclusions to God's love? Have you held back conversations about God in a specific company? Visualize a flood of limitless proportions destroying all those obstacles and feel connected to Him now. Remember, all limits are placed by mortals.

Your Thoughts

Day 12
Why We Talk Differently About God

Think of the last time you hung out with your friends? Did you gossip about your other friends? Did you discuss the news? Whatever the content of the conversation was, I can almost guarantee that you talked about every topic with similar ease. Whenever a conversation about God comes up, it becomes a different type of conversation. Our demeanor and voices change. How willing others are to listen also changes. For many of us, how willing we are to talk about Him changes. In this chapter, I look at the underlying reasons so we can invite God into all of our lives.

We disconnect God from material.
We are spiritual beings, souls, having a human experience. A lot of human experience depends on the material. This includes material wealth, material reality, and all the problems associated with the two. We have jobs, friends, and drama stemming from these material conditions, but because we see God in a spiritual context, we try to place Him in a box where He isn't a part of any conversation associated with material. Ironically, He is the creator of this material reality which we aren't willing to share with Him.

Remember that in the absence of His word, nothing exists. So start easing Him into your material life. It is the only way to elevate this base reality and make all your material experiences spiritual. No wonder people feel guilty about making money. They exclude God from conversations about money. You can use the money for good. In fact, it is very hard not to use the money for good. Even when you use it for your business, you're serving His children and employing them. When you don't talk about God the same way you do about money, you are
held back from pursuing money.

We prioritize people.
The moment we edit ourselves based on people around us, the people become our prison. Generally, our 'prisons' are comfortable enough that we don't feel confined. For example, if you have some conservative beliefs, but your friends are liberals, you may feel oppressed when you can't openly support a conservative point in their presence. If being a

conservative is your whole identity, you'll feel imprisoned hanging out with these friends.

As a result, we choose our friends based on what we can't help but talk about. If you love sports, you'll find people who love talking about it, and as long as you share that, you can let go of things they don't want to hear about. Many of us have made friendships in times where God wasn't such a huge part of our lives. Now that we invite Him into our lives, we learn that the friends we have aren't as open to those conversations.

Let today be the day where you ask yourself, "Do I prioritize my friends enough to limit my conversations about the Lord?" My humble suggestion is to ease Him into your conversations. Praise Him when you talk about your next promotion. Credit Him when you show kindness to a friend. You don't have to preach to them, just stop censoring God.

Your Thoughts

Day 13:
The Global Average Breath: Understanding Potential

You breathe the same air as I do, and generally speaking, we breathe virtually the same quantity of air. This is a sobering thought in that we have the same source of life and similar potential. When applied to the right area, we can expand it to infinity. That raises a question, if we have the same breath and potential, then why do we not make the same level of progress throughout our lives? I believe a big part of it is our mindset.

We breathe the same air but have a different mindset.
Each one of us has gone through a series of experiences that have shaped our beliefs. Some of us have overcome adversity to have ground-shaking confidence in our abilities to conquer anything. Others have blamed themselves for their circumstance and assumed their lives are meant to be filled with suffering. Some unfortunate souls have blamed God for their circumstances instead of taking their position in life as an opportunity to connect with Him.

How to improve your mindset.
Now that you understand that your mindset defines your experience of life and largely helps shape your future, let's examine the prosperous Christian mindset.

"I will be fine."
While uncertainty and anxiety are a part of being human, that's only because the default human experience lacks faith. When you have faith in the Lord, and you understand that He is capable of taking care of you and is willing to do so, you know in your heart that you will be fine regardless of how tough the circumstances might seem. With the 'I will be fine' mindset, you will no longer worry about things out of your control. You will not panic, and you will not make decisions that may sabotage your own success. To adopt this mindset, always begin your day by thanking God for taking care of you through all of your worst times so far.

"My blessings will multiply."

While our base existence relies on constantly looking out for things to get angry about, dissatisfaction isn't the Christian mode of being. From simplest religious traditions like saying grace, to thanking the Lord upon getting blessed, we have the righteous tendency to thank the Lord in the moment. However, we fail to be thankful for the sum total of our blessings. You may thank God for helping you get a job, but you may forget to thank Him for every paycheck that comes from that blessing. When you adopt the "my blessings will multiply" mindset, you don't fear scarcity and never expect lack. Every time you are blessed, you thank the Lord and expect more blessings.

To adopt this mindset, you must look back at all the ways in which God has blessed you and then thank Him. Do this every day, so you start your day expecting more blessings. When you're grateful, God gives more. Remember, when something may be 'too much' for you, there is no such thing in the eyes of God. So ask your heart's desire and be grateful for every way in which you have been blessed.

Your Thoughts

Day 14:
Everything Must Exist Together

If you go as far back as Genesis, you will realize that the purpose of existence is coexistence. Harmony was first interrupted by the serpent. I believe its ripple effects can be felt to the present moment where we continue to divide and judge. Unfortunately, we aren't able to correct this because we have added righteousness to our division.

While we understand that it is wrong to sow seeds of division and resentment along the lines of race, gender, or nationalism, we have deemed it right to hate our fellow brothers and sisters because they don't share the same religious beliefs as us. Not only does this get in the way of our mission to have the world be a harmonious place, but it also keeps us from ever repenting. Why repent for what you think is right?

We must coexist to influence.
I don't believe you should create social relationships with the intention to convert other people. You must make great friendships for the sake of making friendships. When you genuinely care enough for your fellow brothers and sisters, they understand that any word of God you extend to them comes from a place of good intentions. Do not hold a metaphorical gun to their heads and give them ultimatums to convert. Don't pull back your friendship if they don't agree with your beliefs.

Don't be arrogant.
You know that God works in mysterious ways. You also understand that everyone is a part of God's plan. Suppose you won't reach into your local handyman's toolbox and remove a tool, how can you remove God's tools based on your perspective. You don't know how useful someone you label a "non-believer" might be to the community from which you're willing to exclude them.

That's why you have to be inclusive and keep your arms open. You're open to God's plan when you let those you don't agree with be a part of your life. So don't just tolerate people you disagree with, expect them to be a source of good in your life because you expect the best from the Lord.

Create conditions for genuine belief.

In a dictatorship, the leader doesn't know people hate him till there is a revolution. The epitome of this was in the French revolution, where Marie Antoinette was told that people were protesting because they didn't have bread. She said, "let them eat cake." She had no idea of their lack till it was too late. Oppression breeds dishonesty, and even though you're not putting a gun to someone's head and forcing them to convert, if you start using social pressure and exclusion to push people towards agreeing with you, you rob them of the opportunity to genuinely discover and accept Christ into their lives. You and I don't have the right to do that.

So live and let live. Be a great role model of prosperity and kindness. People will want to know how you are so generous and why you're thriving. When you credit the Lord with your blessings, you will spread His message more effectively. Let today be the day you strike a positive conversation with someone you disagree with.

Your Thoughts

Day 15:
Empathy Paves The Way For Generational Prosperity

From Jacob to Abraham, each story involving progeny shows that God's plan is generational. It means in our lives, we have to stop thinking of a single lifetime and start considering how our attitudes and actions impact generations to come. Our babies deserve parents who think about more than themselves.

At this point, you may want to react and say you care about your children. Unfortunately, we do so in the wrong way. We try too hard to make our kids the best players, but we aren't thinking of the playground. Are we pushing our environment towards destruction? Physically and metaphorically, we are forcing our children's future to be governed by traditions of exclusion and judgment.

We are also doing no favors to the environment. Our consumption practices are creating horrible working conditions. If that becomes the norm, it will also be the economy our grandchildren will be forced to get jobs in. So how will you fix this today?

I believe today can be the day where you reflect on all the ways in which you can preserve the landscape in which your children grow up. Wouldn't you like to create a society not fueled by group tensions? It starts at home.

Children learn from observing, not listening. So, become more empathetic and keep an open mind. Make friends who have those values as well, so your children can hang out in places of positive influence. While you may not change the world and its physical environment, you can change your child's entire world by focusing on tolerance in their upbringing.

I haven't seen a single narrow-minded parent whose children have a happy childhood. How fondly your kids remember their early days is in your control. Are you going to gear them towards success by setting them up with a positive mindset, or are you going to make them perpetual pessimists? You govern their relationship to reality. Furthermore, you decide how they view God.

So help your children expect the best from God.
Help them see that God's on their side, but also that God loves everyone just as they should. It is no use raising kids to be great players if their personalities are so rigid no one wants to play with them.

Teach them to be flexible and then let them be themselves, or should I say let them discover themselves? If you continue to be judgmental towards others, you'll be judgmental towards them as well. As a result, they'll block you out of their lives.

When your children start hiding things from you, they can become vulnerable to others' influence. At this point, it is officially too late. So don't see them as you want them to be. See them as you were at their age. Be open-minded towards their mistakes and lead with empathy. They want to be understood, not idealized, and held to a standard you know is too high for someone their age. Let them relax, so they don't develop unhealthy coping behaviors. Free them up to prosper. If you have kids, talk to them today. If you don't, talk to anyone. Exercise empathy.

Your Thoughts

Day 16
Those You Help Must Want To Be Helped

It is your duty to support certain people like your parents and your children. This, of course, must be done within reason. In general, you must be generous where you can be so you can spread positivity and further the march of prosperity. Today is the day you learn to tell people apart by how deserving they are of your time. This may seem extremely judgmental, but as a soldier marching with the aim to change the world for the better, you are the most useful in helping those who want to be helped.

That is why you must learn to detect early and disengage whenever someone seems to be in need of help but unwilling to listen. It is not your job to improve people's lives with force. When you try to do that, you make them stubborn in their ways and waste precious time and energy that you can be using to help those willing to help themselves. The philosophy of the whosoever-wills is one of keeping an open mind, so you can extend your support and message to anyone. I have no issues with that. You must also keep your eyes open.

When you help someone, and they aren't grateful, that's fine. You did not help them to gain their thanks. You helped them for the Lord's sake, but when you try to help someone and they remain in their cycle doing the things that put them in their current situation, you have to opt-out.

Questions to ask when helping others.
Before you sign up to be the shoulder on which someone cries, or you can offer to help out with physical work or anything else, ask the person who needs your help what they will do differently to avoid being in the same place again. That's because your priority is moving forward. When you move forward and bring them along with you, it's splendid. It's impossible for you to be attached to them and move forward while they're moving in a circle.

Ask them what they'd do differently, because it's better than asking them what their role in their current position is. When you ask someone "What's your part in this?", they feel personally attacked and

get defensive. It also isn't helpful because it isn't solution-oriented thinking. Instead, when you ask, "So what's your role in this?", they start thinking differently. You help them position their own
problems like a puzzle, and we love a good puzzle.

    Today you must reflect on your social circle and silently group them into those who'd love to help themselves and those who move in circles. You must love them all but must only offer help to those willing to help themselves. Also, keep an open mind because you never know when someone insisting on a cyclical existence is suddenly ready to get set and join the march. Remember that this is regarding your approaching people to help. When someone comes to you seeking help, they've already decided they need help. You must help as much as you can, but in going up to people and trying to help them, avoid the ones not willing to help themselves or even admit they need help.

Your Thoughts

Day 17:
Base Nature vs. Spiritual Nature: What Is Your Truth?

The rise of science has also contributed to the narrative of the animalistic human. Our sublime nature has been discounted with excessive emphasis on what we have in common with mammals in general, but this isn't a surprise to religion. We have always known that humans have a base nature, but we acknowledge that they also have a higher nature.

Science, in its insistence on materialistic analysis, ignores our spiritual nature. As long as we can experience it, we know it exists. In this chapter, we will look at both sides of our nature. This day won't be one where you decide you are one or the other. It will be the day you figure out how to resonate with a higher frequency and elevate your vibe.

Our nature is dictated by emotions.
Of all the things, ironically, it is our emotions that govern how spiritual or animalistic we are. A person who grows up in abundance has an easier time being generous. On the other hand, the person in a position of so much scarcity that he can barely fend for himself has little to no room for empathy. Of course, exceptions exist and there are inspiring examples like that of the widow's mite.

Jesus loved to witness people perform noble acts and that's why once He was sitting opposite to the treasury watching people donate. The wealthy were donating large sums but among the donors was a widow. She had two mites (worth a few cents in today's currency). She polished them with her cloth and placed them in what was by now a small heap of coins and currency. Jesus said to His companions that many had donated that day, but the woman's donation was worth all of the others' combined. That is not materialistic math, that's the emotion given weight. The donors had all given from their surplus, but the woman had given all she had.

This lesson teaches us that one's nature isn't dictated by circumstance but by mindset. While most donors have a mindset of abundance once they have enough money to feel secure, the widow trusted God enough to give all she had because she knew God would take care of her.

I believe this gives us the distinction between emotions that bring us to our animal nature and emotions that bring us to our spiritual nature. Faith in God helps us transcend. Security, certainty, and confidence are all emotions that elevate you towards your spiritual nature. On the other hand, fear and panic make you more of a human-animal. So, think about 2020, how have we all behaved? Collectively, the toilet-paper hoarding, the penny-pinching, and business owners' mass-firing of employees prove that we opted to relate more to our animal side than our spiritual side. Why don't we flip it today? Why don't you flip it today? There is no exercise for the day. All you have to do is trust God and have faith that tomorrow will be better.

Your Thoughts

Day 18:
If You Can Make A Difference, You Should Make A Difference.

Since time changes, everything changes in relation to it. For example, a kid who learns to crawl before the age of one is considered a fast-learner. If that's all he learns and enough time passes, he would be a five-year-old who only crawls. At that point, he'd be considered slow. This applies to everything, including money. If you have a million dollars that stays a million for fifty years, you will have half the buying power. The point is that things staying the same is an indicator of the situation getting worse. We must always move forward.

Someone has to make a difference, or everything stays the same. As you know by now, that's not good. So who will make the difference? Well, people who can't make a difference can't do so, that only leaves behind people who can. That's where my position emerges, if you can make a difference, you should make a difference. It is easy to look at a billionaire and say, "That person is capable of feeding a million poor people, he should feed a million poor people". This only serves to distract you from the fact that you can feed ten starving people. Ten of God's children making a difference counts than watching someone else's wallet.

Today, I want you to commit to watching your own abilities. Look at what you can do with your time, money, and skills to make a positive difference in the world. Do not let the standard of difference be so high that you are discouraged from taking a small step—every small step matters.

The modern internet culture has given rise to the idea that everything has to be larger than life. That's not the case with positive change. Refusing to act unless your action makes a global change overnight is like refusing to get a job as a fresh graduate unless you get paid a million dollars. That's just a recipe for progress-stopping paralysis.

So what is the solution? In my estimation, you should focus on what you can do. It starts with a smile and a compliment and, if you stick with this philosophy it results in changing the world. A kind

word from you might be all that a stranger needs to carry on living. Do not underestimate the impact of
a small act of kindness.

    As your exercise for the day, I'd like you to sit with a pen and paper and compile a list of positive things you can do. Write down Twenty-five items on this list as our goal is to stretch our minds and explore opportunities for making a difference that we usually overlook. You can pay for the person behind you in line at the coffee shop. That will help someone start their morning in a good mood. By now, you understand what I mean by small acts that make a big impact. Make a list of twenty-five and do one of the acts today.

Your Thoughts

Day 19:
Belief Is Having The Courage To Speak and The Patience To Listen

I feel the need to pen a chapter on belief precisely because our current concept of it is not right. We treat belief as a "Private Thing" where we hold certain opinions and silently reject everything that doesn't align with them. Holding such beliefs is a low-risk way of having well-defined opinions. Belief is something that moves you and for something to move you in a way that matters, it has to move you enough to publicly profess what you think.

I believe that any belief you hide from those whose opinion you care about isn't a belief. It is a hypothesis. Just like a kid who is unsure about his answer doesn't shout it out in class while the one who believes he is right does, the true believer is comfortable saying what he believes. This must make many readers pause. Have we treated our belief in Jesus as a hypothesis?

I want you to start talking about God, religion, and church with as much comfort as you talk about clothes you like. Silence comes from doubt. Don't let your doubt over others' reactions spill into your belief in our savior. Someone once said, "Don't let the people who didn't die for you become a higher priority than the one who did."

With that said, I don't want you to force your beliefs on everyone around you. A chocolate cake tastes amazing, but when you force-feed it to someone who is full, you only make them throw up, and they definitely don't get to enjoy it. Faith in God is a gift. Do not make others reject it because of your attitude. Let people desire it by the way you carry yourself. When I say you must be public about your belief, I mean you should not be hesitant to associate yourself with Christ. Talk about your relationship with God and your faith in Him. Don't have any shame about it. That's the essence of belief.

"But wouldn't my friends not want to hang out with me?" you may wonder. If your openness is one-way, then sure, they will feel like they have to distance themselves from you. Many churches preach that this is alright. I don't believe it is. Antonio T. Smith, a friend and mentor, deals with people of all faiths. He's very open about what he believes, and he lets people express and stand by their beliefs. As a result, Antonio has attracted a following spanning millions of people. If he can have Hindus, Muslims, Sikhs, and Buddhists follow him while being openly Christian, you can keep your friends close while being open about your beliefs.

Just remember to let them be open about what they believe, and they'll be okay with you standing by your beliefs. Those who love to silence the opposing view are afraid of it. True belief is having the courage to speak and the patience to listen. Today is the day you start cultivating that. So, ask one of your friends about his or her beliefs. Listen to them and then let them know whether you agree or disagree. Don't try to prove anything. This will allow you to be open about what you believe without receiving push-back.

Your Thoughts

Day 20:
The Significance and Reality Of Jesus

On paper, Christianity is the fastest-growing Religion. Today, we go beyond the title of Christianity or the label of Christian and explore the reality of Christ. One does not need to be a Christian to recognize that Jesus existed. There is historical data, and archaeologists have found multiple locations referred to in the bible. Unlike King Arthur, who was first mentioned five hundred years after his supposed passing, Jesus is mentioned in historical accounts of the time when He walked the Earth.

If Jesus existed in reality, was he just a man later elevated by legend? We believe He is the Son of God and performed miracles in no metaphorical sense. For He had the physical abilities to heal, love, and sacrifice beyond human comprehension. It is important to separate faith and knowledge. The gap that is meant to be filled by faith will never be filled by knowledge.

Now we can see historical accounts of Jesus. Not so long ago, atheists denied every account in the bible as fiction, but upon uncovering the remains of the pool of Bethesda where Jesus healed a paralytic (a place atheists previously said didn't even exist), they have shifted their stance. Now they say the pool exists, but the book that referred to it hundreds of years after it was buried, just got lucky.

As you may have realized, atheists will not be convinced of any new position by learning more about Jesus. That's because knowledge is a tool, not the goal, whereas faith is the goal, not a tool. What is chemistry? It is a pursuit of leveraging chemicals for our betterment. All knowledge in chemistry is meant to further us along this journey. Similarly, physics is our attempt to uncover the laws that govern material processes so we can use them to make our lives longer and more convenient. All knowledge is acquired with an intent. That is why, whether you find Jesus or not, doesn't depend on the amount of knowledge you have but your intention, and to intend to believe in the Son of God is faith.

So, why do people try so hard to refuse Jesus? I believe it is because of low self-esteem. It requires a lot of self-respect to believe that one is worth saving. If someone does not have enough self-esteem and thinks negatively about himself/herself, it is impossible for him/her to fathom that the Son of God sacrificed Himself to save them.

Your guideline for the day is to stop arguing on the basis of knowledge and material facts in order to "prove" Jesus. Instead, work on raising people's self-esteem by treating them with respect and kindness. When people love themselves enough and believe they are worthy of God's love, they'll open themselves up to Christ. You must be patient. This also applies to yourself. If you have faith in the Lord, be thankful but if your faith falters every now and then, work on raising your self-esteem so you can get steadfast in your belief.

Your Thoughts

Day 21:
Learn Something Different, and It Will Make All The Difference

Positive progress is the result of accommodating the change. Today, we will uncover the philosophy of appreciating differences and the one thing that makes all the difference. First, let's discuss what makes people cling to the "same." If you notice, most resistance in your life comes from insisting on keeping things the same. How helpful is that?

Of course, this only frustrates you because things never stay the same. By resisting change, you might block the possible blessings God is sending your way. Your resistance may delay the fruits you seek. If you become more open to change, you can make sure the change is positive. People resist change because they believe what they have is the best they can get. Even those supposedly unhappy with their circumstances believe their "horrible" situation is the best they can have. Self-esteem determines so much in life.

At least learning about this can encourage you to raise your self-esteem. Be around people who elevate you. If you have shared this book with your friends and they have read up to the previous chapter, they're working on their self-esteem as well. This will bring about a collective positive.

While you learn about your taxes and side-incomes and create a positive difference with each piece of knowledge, I urge you to learn more about Christ. Learning anything different about Him leads to a positive leap. These instantaneous leaps can heighten your spiritual experience of life.

Jesus needed alone time.
For a long time, people have been boxed into 'extrovert' and 'introvert' categories. Our personal experience of social life shows that it is

impossible to always want company or solitude. A comforting fact about Jesus may help you understand yourself better. Jesus needed to withdraw from crowds to reflect in peace and solitude. Eremos Cave is cited as one of the locations where He would spend such periods. In your life, you can make 'social detox' a thing and derive the benefits of superior mental processing and inner peace.

Jesus was considered a radical.

If you feel like you don't fit in with the times, fret not. At His time, Jesus was seen as a radical for talking to sinners and having conversations with
women. Moreover, there's the fact that He let people pick grain on the Sabbath. Don't let others'
judgments define how you conduct yourself. Do what you believe is right, and you will go farther than you will while seeking everyone's approval.

Jesus asked for what he wanted.

Whenever you find yourself suffering in silence, remember that the Lord professed His thirst multiple times when going through the six hours of agony and taking away our sin. Knowing that the roman soldiers were no allies of his, he still
professed His thirst. "I am thirsty" and "I thirst" are two quotes noted by biblical scholars who find them to fulfill prophecies. It is also worth noting that Jesus, even in His most vulnerable moment, did what was in His control to get into the best position. He professed His thirst, had His lips moistened, and with a little boost in strength proclaimed: "It is finished." You have no reason not to ask for support or help now that you have the example of the Lamb of God.

Today, you've learned three lessons, but this day is meant for you to start the practice of learning more about Christ. There is a treasure trove of insightful knowledge about Him, and everything you learn makes a difference.

Your Thoughts

Day 22:
Understand That God Is Grand

People have tried to put God in a box. Some have tried to do so to make sense of Him, and others have attempted this in the hopes of gaining power over others. Today, I want you to understand that God is grand. He is bigger than people. He is bigger than institutions, and He is bigger than your understanding. So what does this mean for your life?

It means you must extend your limits of tolerance when you try to picture God's tolerance. When you try to understand His forgiveness, don't even dare compare it with the human concept of forgiveness. Many people avoid seeking forgiveness only because they feel guilty for repeatedly repenting after sinning over and over. While this would frustrate a human, God has infinite mercy and a capacity for forgiveness that knows no limits.

Understand that all the knowledge and understanding of pastors, priests, and churches combined does not cover even a single percent of what there is that you don't know about God. In the larger picture, even the church doesn't know God in His entirety. Let no institution, no group, and no individual keep you from developing a relationship with God in a way that feels right to you.

As long as you believe in Jesus and form the relationship through acknowledgment of the sacrifice that cleans us of sin, there is no person in the world to get between you and God. Jesus took your sin the same way He took mine. He came to Earth to sacrifice for you as much as He came for the most pious person you can imagine. Please, do not let your opinion of people's virtue lead you towards placing them on a pedestal where they can tell you about limits to God's tolerance, mercy, and forgiveness.

There are many who will keep you from associating with people who don't believe in Jesus. Many will judge you for having 'sinner' friends.

There is no shortage of people who will tell you that your entire life is filled with nothing but sin. Listen to none of them. Your heart will tell you which pastor is providing the best reflection. Your soul will vibe with the right group. Let your gut guide you, because when you give yourself to Christ, God
connects you to the people you must connect with.
Today is the day you let go of your previous
limiting beliefs and be open to forgiveness, social
connections, and opportunities in Jesus' name.

Your Thoughts

Day 23:
Lessons Learned Talking To A Muslim About Jesus

Did you know that Muslims believe in Jesus? That is why I stand by talking to people who have a different belief. It is not about changing your own or their minds. It is about understanding things about others that correct what you assume about them. We don't want to be judged by wrong assumptions, so why should we judge others like that? In this chapter, I will convey what I learned from coming in contact with a Muslim.

Muslims believe Jesus was the Messiah.

Many of my readers may have heard that Muslims consider Jesus a messenger of God. I did not know they consider Jesus to be the Savior. They believe in Mohammad as the final prophet, but they believe it is Jesus' God-given duty to save humanity. They even believe in the Savior's second coming.

One can't be a Muslim if he rejects Jesus.
Believing in Jesus is essential to be a Muslim. We can be Christian without believing in their prophet, but they have to believe in Jesus to qualify as Muslims. They have immense respect for Jesus and believe Christians are the closest to them in the sense that there is only a minor difference in beliefs. However, there is a difference in practices.

Muslims believe in virgin birth.

Let's now unpack some differences where the belief systems diverge. Unlike atheists and even some 'Non-practicing' Christians who see the bible as a metaphor, Muslims believe in the miracle of the virgin birth. However, they believe the birth occurred through the will of God and does not make Jesus God's begotten son.

Islamic view of the crucifixion.

Aside from believing in Jesus as a human prophet, Muslims also differ from us in belief when it comes to sacrifice on the cross. They believe in intentions equal in weight of actions. Mohammad said, "Actions are but by intentions." As a result, they believe that for Jesus to intend to sacrifice Himself was enough. According to their belief, Jesus was lifted by God to the heavens and will come back as humanity's Savior to fight the Antichrist with the army of the righteous. They believe Roman soldiers were placed in a divine trance where they crucified Judas instead.

While that seems like a happy ending, unfortunately, it doesn't make sense.
- If Jesus was lifted to the heavens, why was there a need to have an imitation Christ take the punishment?
- Even if the intention to sacrifice counts, it is six hours of continuing to intend to suffer for our sins that add weight to Jesus' sacrifice. Believing in last-minute attention takes away that weight.

In conclusion, I do not agree with Muslims' beliefs regarding Christ, and I don't hate Muslims for what they believe. I'm glad I know more about how they view the Lord. It helps me not judge them unfairly. I hope you start learning more about others' views and maintain your ability to stay solid in your beliefs. When you can exist as a Christian among publicly Muslim, Jewish, and Hindu people, your belief is sufficiently solid.

We can't forget that Ishmail was Abraham's first seed. This is what we must embrace moving forward.

Your Thoughts

Day 24:
How To Turn Your Life Into A Feel-Good Movie

At one point in 2019, everyone started saying, "2020 is going to be like a movie," and "in 2020, my life will be a movie." By March 2020, we realized that we forgot to pick the genre. Generally, when we say we want to live in a movie, we didn't mean a horror flick. In this chapter, we are going to go over the one thing that can help you turn your life into a feel-good movie.

What's an anxious flick?

Whenever you watch a horror movie, a mystery, or a thriller, at the most engaging times, your gut is in a knot. These are the movies you don't want to
watch because while their uncertainty is engaging, having that kind of unpredictability in your life would be highly stressful. The opposite of these movies are feel-good flicks.

What are feel-good flicks?

Feel-good movies are the ones where you know things will work out. There is a moment of tension, but you have confidence it will be resolved, and something better will come from it. To make feel-good movies feel even better, some of us love
to re-watch them. The re-watch allows you to be even more comfortable because you know exactly how it will end.

How your life can be like a feel-good movie

To be in a feel-good flick, you must borrow similar certainty into your real life. The number one
way to add certainty to your life is to trust in God completely. When you believe in God so fully that you start seeing your life as a viewer, it will become a feel-good movie.

No moment of "uncertainty" will ever have your gut in a knot, because you trust God to take you to better places, even when something bad happens. Then you will have faith that something so great will come out of it that you'll thank God for the "bad" thing as it will become a door to excellence you cannot even imagine.

Use momentum to get in the motion-picture frame.
We think and experience narratives. To get into the movie mindset, you must hop out of your default mindset. For this, I'll outline a meditation you should try today.
- Find yourself in a distraction-free environment and sit in a comfortable position.
- Start remembering the best moments of your life so far. Do so in detail and see yourself as the main character.
- Imagine movie music playing in the background as you recall moments from your life.
- Remember getting out of tough situations and getting saved by 'chance' from potential worst-case scenarios.
- Imagine a credit overlay saying, Directed by God.

This meditation will put you in the mindset of being a protagonist in a movie. All you have to do after this is trust God completely, and do what is
evidently the best for yourself and your fellow brothers and sisters.

Your Thoughts

Day 25:
If You're good At Being Bad, The Enemy Will Be Mad

My show "D Block Church" has followers and listeners from all over the world. That means different sayings, different teachings, and different episodes are remembered by different people for different reasons. That is why it is worth noting when a single quote becomes popular with almost everyone in my audience. One such saying is, "If you're good at being bad, the enemy will be mad." A large contributor to the saying catching on is that it rhymes. So, I am writing this chapter to elaborate on its meaning. If you were good in your sin, the "Enemy" will fight hard to keep you in it.

All progress is hindered by being afraid to be bad.
People often over-think about how people will view them if they were to fail at something. From trying your hand at piano to becoming good at sketching, you have to start by being bad. If there's anything that will make your enemies happy, it's your fear of being bad. So, my response is to flip it. If you try something and are good at it in the first go, you oughta be disappointed with the kind of target you picked. It is evident from the first results that you picked something too easy. Do only the things you're initially bad at it. Being bad is a barometer of progress. If you start off bad, you can get better, but if you start off 'okay,' well, the average is the enemy of excellence. Furthermore, being bad is an exercise in confidence. "But how is being bad an indicator of confidence?" It shows confidence in your future self. "I may not be great at this, but in the future I got this," you say when you dare to try something you're bad at.

So, let today be the day you dare to try to suck at something. But I will not push you to do that alone. Here are some pointers that will make you good at being bad.

- **Compare yourself to the "you" from yesterday** –
The most helpful thing when taking up a new skill or progressing in any area is to

avoid comparing yourself to external models and compare yourself to the "you" from yesterday.

- **Don't judge yourself for being bad –** Negative self-talk kills more dreams than any obstacle. If you try something and realize you sucked the first time, see it as just that: the first time. Don't multiply failure with forever and give up.
- **Get excited about failing –** When you try something and fail, get excited. "Why should I get excited?" I hear you say.

Simple: failure is an important yet painful step at the beginning of your journey. Be

excited that you got it out of the way.

Always remember when it gets really bad like turbulence, please know that means you are close to your destination.

Your Thoughts

Day 26:
What We Are Fighting: Uncertainty and Threats To Faith

I am blessed to have the audience that I have, and I thank the Lord every single day for each one of you. Together, we are fighting the good fight but do we even know what we are fighting for? We are fighting for a sense of confidence that emerged from trusting God. We are fighting for the certainty that comes from solid faith. The enemy is uncertainty because it makes humans gravitate towards their bad nature. We are fighting this battle to preserve faith so that goodness shall prevail.

My message has been to be on your march, get set, and go. Though I have chapters dedicated to each one of those ideas, I want this chapter to represent my mission. I want to turn every listener of my show, every reader of my books, and every member of my audience into a distributor of certainty. I want to shut the shops of the merchants of doubt who make you feel bad. The whole planet will become collectively confident when we are done with our mission.

As you know, I can't do this alone. Whether you contribute by dialing into my show or with a kind word on my social media, you are a part of this. I want you to extend your support to our cause by opening up your own shop. Yes, I want you to become a distributor for this franchise of certainty. Please extend support and confidence to anyone you come in contact with. Let people know that as they've been fine through all of their worst moments before, they'll be fine in the future. Help people with what you've learned over the past month and help with the planet's healing.

From news media to opportunist politicians, everyone is willing to exploit fear, anger, and uncertainty to turn humans into predictable animal packs they can leverage for their own goals. Help humanity break free by spreading certainty. Every person you come in contact with is a person you can free. All you have to do is tell them, "They'll be alright, everything will be fine."

More importantly, stay strong in your faith. When you have faith, nothing can shake you. This kind of confidence is inspiring for those watching from afar. Before you know it, they're watching up close. As you are open about your beliefs, they understand that your faith in Jesus is helping your mindset. That's when they too see the light. Whether you help people rediscover Jesus, convert to Christianity, or just smile on a sad day, you're doing God's work. Remember He loves all His children, and you cannot apply human discrimination to the limitless love of God.

Last but not least, your faith will be tested. There will be situations so uncertain that your logical mind will find nothing to grasp at. Those are the moments where you can cling to faith and give it no choice but to get stronger, or abandon it and live a life of anxiety. My advice is that you trust God completely.

Your Thoughts

Day 27:
How To Be On Your March

I once started an episode of D Block Church by saying, "On Your March, Get Set, Go". So many people were like, "Wait, isn't that on your marks?" That was an intentional play on words because I genuinely mean we have to be together. "On your marks" is the beginning of a race where we try to outrun each other. "On your march" is the call to march together towards a common goal, as mentioned in the last chapter, our goal is to spread certainty and fight doubt. Today, we will discuss the best practices of being on your march.

Communicate clearly

When working with others, you have to stop assuming they already know what's in your head. This is a natural tendency that we must fight by communicating whatever is important, even if it may seem evident. You'll not march alone. You'll be accompanied by everyone else you'll persuade to join you on this journey of confidence and certainty. As you fight doubts and faith-shaking tests, you'll have to be very clear about your feelings, beliefs, and values.

Designate and delegate

While the general idea of spreading certainty is the mission of God Got Goons, I leave you free to decide the best way of spreading certainty. Some of our members buy meals for the homeless. This stops the uncertainty regarding where their next meal will come from. Others help kids study for their exams. Again, this makes students certain that they'll get better marks. As you decide how your group (family, friends, etc.) can spread certainty, you'll have to assign roles. Give roles based on people's strengths and interests. Remember, this is going to be the largest voluntary march on the planet.

Be forgiving

Forgiveness is very important in fostering collaboration. If you march with high standards, humans are sure to fall short every now and then. Being a true leader means you will forgive and understand. The last thing you want is to make personal judgments based on errors. We don't want to be remembered for our wrongs.

Get people excited.

There is no march for waking up at 5:00 AM in the morning. That's because it is not a universally
exciting idea. When you're marching for your goal, you'll actively be recruiting. While certainty is nice, you can't get people excited about it without
painting a specific picture. So get in touch with your inner artist and paint the most beautiful picture to
get people on board.

Don't give up

You must remember that there will be days where you will feel like giving up. You might think, "What am I doing?" but I urge you to return to this book. Remember that by fighting doubts and spreading certainty, you're making faith and spirituality more accessible to everyone. Remember that this is a worthy goal, and you're not alone. You're on a march, and you've got allies.

Your Thoughts

Day 28:
How To Get Set

If you've skipped to this part, boy, you have missed a lot. We are in full momentum towards changing the future and turning the Earth into a place more accommodating of faith. Yes, we're marching towards a future of certainty, confidence, joy, and positivity. We're trusting God completely to make our mission a success. You have to get ready. You have to get set.

Make a list of opportunities.

The first part of preparing for your march is to make a list of ways in which you can further certainty and confidence. How can you fight doubt? Are there people in your life who look up to you? If the answer is yes, then you're blessed. The easiest thing you can do is be a pillar of certainty for them. If you want a handy hack to help you discover opportunities to do good, simply ask yourself, "Where is the most doubt and uncertainty around me?" and simply become the tool that removes this uncertainty.

Take inventory of assets.

Ever heard of someone going to war without a war chest? While the analogy might be too on the nose for some people, I am serious about fighting doubt. So I urge you to make a list of your assets. What qualities, connections, and skills can you bring to the table as we move forward in our mission to spread positivity? Can you lend a listening ear? Can you grant guidance or give advice? For many, a monetary donation is a very easy way to contribute, but as our mission is holistic, you'll be furthering the cause in all areas of your life. Therefore, you must make a list of assets in personality, connections, and material possessions.

Create a strategy.

The beauty of our mission is that it serves no one but every soldier on the path. The good you do will make you feel good and the positivity you spread will make your life better. That's why you're the best strategist for your path on our march. Now that you have the list of opportunities to do good and a sense of the things you can use to do good. You must create a strategy to do the most good you can. It is your duty to leverage every talent, skill, and asset granted to you by God. Serve Him with what He has given you. Become what He uses to spread confidence and certainty. Let's elevate our species and have the collective consciousness resonate with a spiritual ring.

Your Thoughts

Day 29:
How To Go

They say that when the going gets tough, the tough get going. That's my inspiration for writing this book. It is 2020, and all its tests remind me of the resilience of the human spirit. It solidified my faith in God, and it made me want to help my audience march towards a bright future. If you've read this far, you're already on the march with me. Let me formally welcome you. You are on a journey towards infinite positivity, towards abundance, and towards giving yourself to God in faith, trust, and love. All I have left for you are a few words on how to keep going.

Things might not go as 'you' planned.

You have certain expectations. It is impossible for us to operate without expectations, but that can be a trap. When things don't go according to what you projected, you might be tempted to abandon the mission. Remember, you can't stop going because time keeps marching, so you are never in the same place. You're always on the move, but if you stick to the mission, at least you're moving towards a noble goal.

Unexpected paths will emerge.

The future is full of invisible doors, each one of them is an opportunity to keep going. You must trust Him to open the right one for you. Please do not ignore opportunities when you tunnel vision on a prior iteration of your plan. Remember that God's plan is senior to yours, and you don't know God's plan. You must trust Him to make the next steps evident for you. That's the ultimate exercise in faith and courage.

You will meet allies.

While being open to unexpected opportunities is one thing, you must also be open to unexpected connections. They say that a majority of success comes not from 'what' events but from 'who' events. This means you win by meeting people. A start-up wins not by 'what' it has on its desks or in its warehouse, it wins by "who" chooses to invest. That's why you must expect God to send you whoever He needs you to come in contact with. Leverage the lessons in this book regarding persuasion, connection, and granting the benefit of the doubt.

    In conclusion, when you are on the go, what counts is how long you keep going. You'll encounter challenges, opportunities, and people. In all of that, you must remain steadfast in your beliefs and committed to your vision. Spread positivity by
eliminating doubt. Help people feel certain about
the future, no matter how different their beliefs are
from yours. Don't put God in a box, and don't let
anyone come in between you and Christ. As long as
you keep these in mind, you'll keep going to the
destination that matters.

Your Thoughts

Day 30:
God Got Goons - Is That You?

Now that we have arrived at the last day of the month, or your last day reading. You are ready to pour into someone else. Yes, this is the final day! I am sure you may be wondering about the term God Got Goons, well I am proud to say that today you have gained Goon status. Prepare yourself for war, but remember the battle is not yours, it's the Lord's. The thing we as Goons understand is that together we stand and divided we'll fall. We also agree that we must share a message, a way of life, and love. Unity!

The power to survive is a power from within that penetrates darkness and negativity. Understanding and believing helps you through all situations. When things are horrible all around you, you will not be moved. This includes being in despair, getting knocked down or experiencing setbacks. This confidence stems from faith and believing that God is right there. It is so powerful when things are working together in harmony.

Some of the best moments of my life involved other people different from me. This is what we Goons do, we allow our light to guide people to Christ. We do this because in a world which presents so many options God will do what He wants, how He wants, when He wants to, using exactly who He wants to. To do exactly what He has for them to do. Doing all that so everyone will know He is real.

That's Goon!

Everything breathing has the potential to reach Goon status. There is a choice to make, a change in how you see yourself. Be the instrument that's willing to get in the trenches and fight this thing with a unified team, that's my dream, I see God Got Goons as my team and we can see this through together. If you know what I mean, join me in this march.

Your Thoughts

Epilogue:
You always have a home

This book started as a stream of consciousness talk on one of my D-Block episodes. I felt the need for there to be a common march towards a positive goal. As I pondered over the principles and values I've stood by since the inception of D-Block Church, I formed a template that can help any believer recenter his belief in the most uncertain times. COVID-19 and 2020, in general, might not be as much of a surprise as we move forward; but chaos is always around the corner. That is why I wanted to turn my conversation "On Your March, Get Set, Go." into a timeless book that can help you anytime there is uncertainty on a global scale or chaos in your personal life. You always have guidance in this book, but more importantly, you have a home in God's Kingdom. Let Him be your source for spiritual content. He is informative, insightful, and He allows life to be entertaining. Let this be my formal invitation to join me as we march forward saving God's Kingdom on MsUnderstood Adrienne on YouTube and TikTok and Adrienne Allen on Facebook.

About the Author

Adrienne M. Allen known as MsUnderstood Adrienne can easily be considered your favorite Auntie or everyone's coolest cousin. A true Proverbs 22:6 child. Adrienne is living proof that all things work together for the good and bad for those who love God and are called for His purpose. MsUnderstood Adrienne is embracing life by removing the masks allowing one's differences to be the glue that unites us together, making the most common thing shared between us the way we breathe. The voice and originator of D-Block Church for the whosoever wills on internet radio. Aside from widespread acclaim for her style of hosting and motivating, Adrienne is also appreciated for her alternative take on religion, which has made Christianity more accessible to a variety of people, especially those who feel excluded by self-important institutions. She is dedicated to being the example of Christ on earth. The singer, songwriter, musician, thespian and now author Adrienne has taken good days and bad days to show Gods' mercy and grace and let the whole world see Gods' face. Adrienne continues to serve as a religious influence in her community. Join Adrienne's community by following "God Got Goons" on all social media.